ABC's
OF FAITH

ABC's
OF FAITH

Rickey Singleton

© Copyright 1991 — Rickey Singleton

All rights reserved. No part of this book may be reproduced or transmitted in any form or by any means, electronic or mechanical, including photocopying, recording or by any information storage and retrieval system without written permission from the author with an allowance being made only for brief excerpts to be used in reviews.

Companion Press
P.O. Box 351
Shippensburg, PA 17257-0351

ISBN 1-56043-477-5

For Worldwide Distribution
Printed in the U.S.A.

Contents

Acknowledgment
Dedication
Preface

Chpt.		Page
1	What Faith Is, What Faith Is Not	1
2	The Faith Walk	13
3	Actions	21
4	Belief	37
5	Confidence	53
6	God Can Be Trusted	65

Acknowledgement

My Sincere Thanks:

To my mentor Dr. Frederick K.C. Price, a man of exceptional character, fortitude, wisdom and understanding. He is a man who delights himself in the privileges and benefits of being in right relationship with our Heavenly Father God. I thank him because his fine caliber of teaching and revelation knowledge brought me into a newness of life far beyond that which I had known. At one time, I was totally defeated in all aspects of life. Now I am blooming and radiant with great success, numerous victories, and prosperity that is ever-present with me. There is no doubt that he is called, anointed, and appointed by God to set the nation free. Thank God I am part of that freedom.

Without Frederick Price sharing the Ever Increasing Faith message, there probably would not be an ABC's OF FAITH by Rickey Singleton.

Pastor Price, you are someone special to me and my ministry.

Dedication

This book is dedicated to Darryl Cannon, my best friend, the one that has truly been closer than a brother to me. Elijah had his Elisha. Paul had his Silas and I have Darryl. Thanks for your loyal support and love.

Pastor Rickey Singleton

Preface

It is essential for believers to know what faith is. If we know what faith is, then we will recognize what faith is not. There are distinct differences between the two. Sometimes the difference is defined only by a "thin line" but crossing over it could be the distinguishing factor between forfeited blessings and an overflowing abundance of God's blessings. If a person doesn't perceive the authenticity of faith, he or she may be inclined to think certain things are "of faith" but they actually deter the faith process. If the enemy (satan) can blind you to the point that you are ignorant of God's Word pertaining to faith, it could result in defeat, sickness and an inferior state of being.

This teaching can be described as revolutionary and "revelationary". It is thought provoking and definitely scriptural. Some believers need their minds released from old religious rhetoric and traditions of men. These things have been depriving and decaying the development of believers to a mountain-moving faith built upon the rock of revelation spoken of by Jesus (Matthew 16:18). Believers should be luminous. Jesus said, "Ye are the light of the world." We should be so radiant and dynamically full of life that the noonday sun would back up and take a bow, paying homage to the light of the Lord and the salt of the earth that we possess. Some believers' light is so dim that it could not outshine a lone Christmas mini-light buried in the bush in the deepest, darkest jungle. The reason being of indicative of a lack of faith. Faith is required for enlightenment and also to receive revelation knowledge, wisdom, understanding and truth by the pre-eminent teaching of the Holy Ghost.

These evident truths are brought to your awareness not to be derogatory but because I utilize the authority given to me by Jesus Christ to admonish and perfect believers. We must be renewed by going through a purifying transformation. Just as a lump of coal after its transformation can become a diamond, exquisite, impeccable, refined and brilliantly unique, let's become what Jesus meant for us to be. Let's accomplish the things He wants us to accomplish through faith!

1
What Faith Is, What Faith Is Not

I've heard several believers give their definition of faith. It has been said, "I acquired faith through the relentless preaching by the preachers and the prayers of the 'mothers of the church' as I occupied a seat on the mourner's bench at the revival meetings. Perhaps the mourner's bench should have been called the 'sinner's hot seat'. I sat there daydreaming until my wandering thoughts were jolted back into reality when I heard a loud, roaring 'SINNER' being hurled at me like lightning. I knew I received faith because I sat there every summer for five years straight. As I looked around, I saw that it was the same group of people sitting on the bench with me each year. Well, after five years of the routine, "I got it." Some say, "My mother prayed with me and I received faith." Others claim to have come into faith "while I was yet a small child sitting on my mother's knee". They say, "Brother Singleton, I have faith." "Well, are you sick?" I inquire. "Yes, but I still have faith. No one can tell me that I don't the faith just because I'm sick!" they adamantly reply.

If you have complete understanding of what faith is and what faith is not, you'll come to a profound realization at the conclusion of this teaching that *faith is current*. It is your present belief concerning circumstances and situations that we're dealt in life. You can manipulate them and make everything work to your advantage by taking charge and changing circumstances man has deemed impossible. You can bring them into the realm of possibility, probability, and ultimately actuality by utilizing faith. Whether you procured the concept of faith twenty years ago or today, faith remains current and active. It will make a present realization of that which you hope to manifest itself some time in the future.

It will be brought into the material earth realm by faith whether the results are immediate or if there is a timely waiting period involved. If the time span is seemingly lengthy, thank and praise God as though you already have it, because you do, by faith. Faith is your present belief.

Some people say, "You speak about this faith is present tense jargon and it deals with the here and now. I have faith and it doesn't have anything to do with the present. It has something to do with what I learned from my mother and also what I learned in Sunday School. I'll have you know that I walked three miles each way through mud, slush and rain to get there and back. I sat on the pew every Wednesday night faithfully and listened to my pastor read that one verse of scripture. He stuck his finger in his ear and started moaning and groaning, and jumping on and off the pews. Then he spun around and fell on both knees. I know he was giving me faith because it felt so good."

Take a critical evaluation of that scenario. Were you really being taught faith or were you taught religion? Are you equating faith with participating in all of those rites, rituals, and traditions handed down from generation to generation? "Faith! Religion! What's the difference?" Satanism is a religion. It results in death and eternal damnation. Faith in Jesus Christ and God's Word (uncensored) is life, peace, joy, prosperity, health and excellence!!

Substance: An Offspring of Faith

*Now **FAITH** is the **SUBSTANCE** of things hoped for, the **EVIDENCE** of things not seen.*

Hebrews 11:1

I want you to pay particular attention to the words *substance* and *evidence*. These two words are the essence or key to receiving an understanding of what faith is and what it is not. The first part of the verse asserts, "Now faith is the *SUBSTANCE* of things hoped for". The word substance in Greek would be defined as tangibility or materiality. Faith causes things to materialize. Faith is the substance of material things that you hope for and evidence or proof of that which cannot be seen. Hope itself has no substance whatsoever. Hope without the application of faith would be just idle thoughts, dreams, or desires that may or may not occur. Remember we are looking for substance, for tangibility through faith in the credence of God's Word. Substance denotes that a thing is in existence. Faith takes that which was only a thought, dream or something that you could not see and makes it visible evidence. Things become manifested in the material earth realm. What is it that you are hoping for today? What is it that you desire? Perhaps it may be a husband or wife, money, joy, etc. To have assuredness about your receiving from the Father of lights, you must develop solidity in your faith walk. If you can grasp these principles, you can rid yourself of hopelessness, limitations and boundaries that have bearing on your receiving and having fullness of joy:

Ask and ye shall receive that your joy may be full.

John 16:24b

Faith Generates Evidence

*Now faith is the substance of things hoped for, the **EVIDENCE** of things not seen.*

Hebrews 11:1

Can you present to me evidence that adhering to the principles of faith stated in God's Word produces the results that you desire?

Evidence is that which serves to prove or disprove something; that which is used for demonstrating the truth or falsity of something. It also serves as grounds for knowing with certainty and believing something with conviction.

Evidence is God's Word. Evidence is the existence of the entire universe and all that is therein. Believers who have their needs met and the desires of their heart are the evidence. People who have been healed and delivered are the evidence.

If faith is the evidence of things that we hope for and are not seen, then the things that we cannot see must be real. If the things were not real, faith couldn't be evidence of the things we cannot see. Faith cannot be the evidence of something that does not exist. The things that cannot be seen must be more real than the things that we can see. Faith says, "Even though I don't see it, it must still exist because The Word of God says I can have the things that I hope for."

Faith is Belief

Faith is belief. The word faith in Greek is the word pistis. The word defined simply means belief. Belief is the mental convictions you acquire from hearing certain things. Now, it has been established that faith is the evidence, faith is the substance, and faith is belief. If you believe and trust in what is written in the Holy Scriptures concerning faith, then you actually have a belief in which the foundation is based upon the immutable Word of God.

I attended a particular church for a long time. Apparently, I didn't know that the doctrine that was being instilled in me would ultimately become my belief. Consequently, I didn't know that which they were teaching would have direct bearing on my succeeding in this life. I didn't know that which they were preaching to me could destine whether or not I would live a life of divine health or die because of sickness or disease in some dreaded hospital room. I didn't perceive that what the minister was preaching to me on Sunday morning was influential in my spiritual development. The Word of

God says that faith is the evidence, faith is the substance, and faith is belief. Whatever you believe is exactly what you will receive. If you confess "I don't believe that I can be healed," that statement breeds finality. It results in your not receiving healing which is a covenant promise to you. Faith produces materiality. I reiterate, whatever you believe that is what you're going to get in this life. If you are affiliated with a church which teaches that you cannot be prosperous, then prosperity will be unattainable and a myth to you. If you are affiliated with a church in which they teach you to struggle, toil, and labor before you obtain anything, you're going to struggle, toil and labor. You'll unfortunately have very little to show for having done so much. On the other hand, if you associate yourself with a church that proclaims that faith is evidence and faith is substance, you can have what you desire based upon The Word of God. The first thing that would happen is that you would develop a hunger for the Word. You would say, "Teach me The Word of God. Teach me that which is going to be a blessing to me throughout my entire life."

There are things to consider in regarding being taught the Word. You can be taught The Word of God and you can be taught how to be defeated with the Word. Undisputably, everything in the Bible comes from God or it comes from men that were inspired by God. Some of these things that are written and are being taught will keep you in bondage. For instance, if you try to live according to the law; if you try to live according to certain guidelines that were given specifically to Israel; if you try to live according to the things foretold in prophecies that don't pertain to the dispensation in which you're living; you will be defeated in life believing The Word of God.

So then faith cometh by hearing, and hearing by The Word of God.

Romans 10:17

Faith comes in a certain package and by a certain vehicle. I want you to understand, faith does not come by experience. Someone said, "Well, I've been in the church for a long time. I've been on this road a long time and haven't gotten tired yet. I'm saved by my Christian experience." Wait a minute! The Word of God never said that faith comes by Christian experience. Faith comes by hearing The Word of God. Your experience can teach you things but faith or belief is better. I prefer to believe a thing based upon that which has already been found to be true rather than experience everything. It has already been documented. It has already been established or proven by a previous source whether or not it is true. My mother taught us when we were small children not to touch the stove. If you touch the stove and it's hot, you will burn yourself. Children don't have to experience that fire is hot and will consequently burn them if they have contact with it. They can see what happened to others who have been burned. There might be scarring or discoloration of the skin that remains. I don't have to experience everything that is written in the Word. I can read it and if I believe, that means I bring God on the scene in the material sense.

If faith comes by hearing The Word of God, it's the Word that builds faith in our lives! We can't actually see the Word. We have to conceive it spiritually and believe it. We're reading it in the book but we're reading words. You cannot actually see words doing the things that they say or being the things that they describe. You can see the selected printed alphabet along with pronunciation put together to form words. The words of God are spirit. In John 6:63, Jesus said, "It is the spirit that quickeneth: the flesh profiteth nothing: the words that I speak unto you, they are spirit, and they are life." In other words Christ was saying, "My words are full of life. My words are alive." When we receive The Word of God, we are receiving life. There is life in the spirit world and life in the Word. Therefore, since faith comes by hearing and hearing by The Word of God, we're receiving life when we hear, believe and absorb the Word.

> *Blessed be the God and Father of our Lord Jesus Christ, who hath blessed us with all spiritual blessings in heavenly places in Christ.*
>
> Ephesians 1:3

I want you to think about this for a moment, my friends. There are some spiritual blessings in heavenly places that are waiting for you. They have your name on them. God has already blessed you with all, not a few of them. I believe that every person in the body of Christ can have all the spiritual blessings. This does not say that one person is supposed to have all of them and another person is not entitled to any of them. I believe the reason why believers don't receive all of them is based upon how much faith they have received by hearing The Word of God. If you hear about the spiritual blessings, then you will know that they are available to you. If you attend a church where the preacher is so preoccupied with what you're going to do for him, friends, you're not going to receive spiritual blessings. The only things you're going to get are an empty pocket, an empty head, an empty heart and an empty life. If you are fellowshipping in a place where they are teaching you the Word befitting the new testament time and grace dispensation in which we are living, you'd better stay there. I don't fault you for having areas of lack in your life, if there happens to be any. I attribute fault to those who say that God has called them to preach the gospel. I'm very hard on preachers because I wasn't preaching the Word. I was teaching that which I heard others preach and that stuff was killing people. It was cursing them to their graves. It was talking about their raggedy lives. Why is it you very rarely go to a church where they tell you who and what you are in Christ Jesus? When I found out that message was not sent of God, I dropped that mess and began to preach The Word of God. God began to bless me. He began to bless all those that came to hear my words that I spoke from His life-giving gospel. An abundant life of faith comes by hearing The Word of God.

I emphatically remind you that faith causes things to materialize. If it is a form of matter that is material, physical, occupies space and is perceived by the senses, no faith is required for it. Faith is the substance of things hoped for and the evidence of things not seen. Faith deals with those things that you cannot perceive. I want you to grasp this. If you can see it, there is absolutely no faith involved! The Word of God reinforces this statement. It requires no faith to purchase a car if you have good enough credit to do so. It requires faith to get the money to make the car payments each month. For instance, you have seen the car that will be sufficient for your immediate needs. You know because of undisciplined spending habits that you don't have the money or the substantial credit rating that is required to obtain the car. Normally it would take very little or no money down to buy an automobile if you have a good credit rating. If your credit picture is somewhat dismal or if you don't have any established credit, it would take the favor of God to intervene by opening the doors for you. It is also possible for you to have an excellent credit rating and not know if you could afford to pay the installments each month. It is a sign of maturity and wisdom to seek direction from the source of our supply, our Heavenly Father, Jehovah Jireh. You may not be able to see exactly how you can afford the car, but Jehovah can and will not only give you favor to help in the time of need, He will create avenues for you also.

By storing the following mental aid in your memory, you can resort back to it in the times you need to exercise faith:

Three Golden Nuggets Of Faith

1. Faith is Belief
2. Faith is Actions based on that Belief
3. Faith is Confidence that the Actions you take will result in bringing forth angels to minister to your needs.

We don't have to sit idly around hoping to receive. If faith is substance, you want substance. You want to touch, feel and see it with your eyes. All that we have to do is envision the things that we need and start "faithing" for them. God, in His infinite knowledge has given man a great developmental tool to utilize called the "mind." With the mind, we are enabled to use the imagination to form mental pictures or ideas. We are able to conceive and create. We are given an imagination so that we can envision ourselves with the things we desire or see circumstances changed with it resulting in our overcoming obstacles and reaping numerous conquests. We are given an imagination to see ourselves actually doing that which we desire to do and accomplishing through our endeavors and faith in God's Word. Seeing these in your mind accentuates realness and concreteness in your walking by faith. Your imagination is to be used for your edification.

2

The Faith Walk

For we walk by faith, not by sight.
II Corinthians 5:7

To walk involves action; to walk is a function that is attributed to living creatures. This verse of scripture is actually saying, in reference to walk, that we *live* by that which we cannot see. People tend to live their lives based upon what their natural senses tell them. They're driven by what they can touch, taste, hear, smell, see or what is dictated to them by their intellect. My friends, people of God, those who are born again, those of us who know that Jesus Christ is Lord, don't walk according to our sensory mechanism. Its components can tell you that Jesus Christ doesn't exist. Your senses can say that you never saw the Lord before. How can you say that He exists? It takes faith to believe that a man named Jesus, who gained notoriety about two thousand years ago, was a true phenomenon. It takes faith to believe that He is coming back. We walk or live by that special understanding of God's Word that has been revealed to us by the Spirit of truth:

Howbeit when he, the Spirit of truth, is come, he will guide you into all truth: for he shall not speak of himself; but whatsoever he shall hear, that shall he speak: and he will shew you things to come.

John 16:13

We walk by faith believing that Jesus is going to come and rapture us away. We believe that God will supply all of our need.

The surroundings that you see tend to dictate certain things to your senses. Your surroundings can suggest to your senses whether or not you are going to obtain that which you desire. Your immediate circumstances will say that you cannot have what you want. You might have gone into an affluent neighborhood and seen beautiful homes. You realize that you only have a minimal amount of money in your bank account. Circumstances enter into your mind and say that you can't afford this. Stay where you are, but you know that you are in need of a newer or better home. The Word expresses that we walk by faith or belief not by that which we can see. When you go into those neighborhoods, you are to find the house that best suits your need and budget. Begin to look at what the Word of God says. You *shall* have what you say. You can walk yourself out of poverty into prosperity by walking according to the Word. You can walk yourself out of fear into faith. You can walk yourself out of doubt into belief. You can walk yourself out of sickness into health.

This is what our life is about, walking by the Word and not by the things we can see. We should be blinded to everything that is going on around us that causes doubt or distrust in our lives. If circumstances should arise that cause you to see a doctor, get the diagnosis from him and become blinded to whatever he has to say contrary to what the Word says pertaining to healing. Doctors and medicine can help you keep things under control until healing manifests. You should say, "If there is something that can keep my blood pressure down, I'm going to use it until I receive my healing manifestation. I believe that I'm healed, not based on the pills that the doctor gives me, but based upon the Word of God." God said, "The sick are made well." We must take a firm stand and say, "I don't see. I'm blinded to the circumstances that befall me." You must become desensitized to what your sensory mechanism dictates to you. Your senses can envelop you and have you accepting extremities that can result in death. People die because their minds tell them they're getting weaker and weaker. You can't handle it. You can't hold on any longer and subsequently they die. The devil cannot kill a born again believer with sickness or disease. You would have had to forfeit your days that God has numbered for you and allow satan to kill you prematurely.

Jesus said that we can have an abundant life that is not founded upon what we feel. Feelings vacillate according to what is going on in our lives. You will not find in the scriptures where Jesus said that by your feelings you are made whole. He never once addressed the issue of feelings. He stayed away from it because He knew that it was the words that proceeded out of His mouth that brought forth healing. In fact, He said, "Your faith has made thee whole." What was their faith? Faith is the substance of things that they were hoping for. Faith took the thing and gave substance to it at that exact moment. The evidence is the words that He was speaking. Whatever Jesus said is what they believed. He would be walking through certain cities and the residents who needed His gift of healing heard that He was coming their way. They desired that He would lay His hands on them. They knew that it took acting on their belief, the belief that the Son of man does have the power to heal. Receiving healing from the Lord is not exclusively based on whether or not you get in the healing line. It's based upon your believing that with his stripes you are healed even before it happens.

> *While we look not at the things which are seen, but at the things which are not seen: for the things which are seen are temporal; but the things which are not seen are eternal.*
>
> II Corinthians 4:18

The first part of the verse tells us not to look at the things or situations that we can see. How do you look not at the things which are seen? The only way you can look not is by closing your eyes. The things that are seen are the things that we see in our direct sight and peripheral vision when our eyes are open. What is it that people see? They see cancer, tumors, poverty, fear, lack, doubt, anxiety, stress, you notice all of those things around you. You can see recessions and depressions. You can see torment. The Bible says, "While we look not at the things which are seen." It is more detailed than that. In most cases, when Paul gave an illustration of a certain thing, he used words that people could identify with.

He's not saying that the only way we can detect in our senses is by sight. We can detect by hearing, tasting, touching, and smelling. While we hear not the things that are being said, while we feel not the things that have touched us, while we look not at the things which are seen, while we taste not the bitterness of things which are bitter, while we smell not the things that have a bad aroma, but look to the things which are not seen. It's imperative for you to start looking at the things you cannot see. That's where some believers have failed. You've been looking at what is right before your eyes. You've been looking in your checkbook at the triple zeros or the quadruple zeros. You say, "They pop up in this book every week. I will never get out of debt." The more you see it, the more you say it and believe it. Faith is the substance of things that we hope for and it's the evidence of things we cannot see. Faith is not the substance of things that we can see or the evidence of things we can feel. When you have your eyes open, you see all of those zeros that show you have a negative balance, but the things you cannot see are the $4,000, the $5,000 or the $10,000 that you desire. You see people dying of cancer or yourself dying of leukemia or arthritis with your eyes open, when you close them, you're healed. When you open your ears, you can hear people telling you that you are dying. When you close your ears, you can't hear negative talk about your death. You can hear that which God is saying to you. He says, "You have life!" You must learn to get away from things you can see and reside in the area of the unseen by utilizing faith.

For the things which are seen are temporal.
II Corinthians 4:18b

The things which are seen are temporary. They come and go. Everything that you see comes and goes. It's the things which are not seen that are eternal. If you want God to bless you with finances now (while you are upon this earth so that you will have financial security until the time you are called to stand in His presence) stop looking at all of the triple zeros and start looking at the banks of heaven. Start looking at God supplying all of your need according to his riches in glory by Christ Jesus:

But my God shall supply all your need according to his riches in glory by Christ Jesus.

Philippians 4:19

Start looking at how God took care of the children of Israel for forty years in the wilderness. Start looking at what the Word says and stop looking at what you see around you. Remember, it is temporary, here today and gone tomorrow. We need to go to a greater source, not a temporary one, but an eternal source which is found in heaven, which comes only by hearing the Word of God. Faith is belief and faith believes what God has said.

But the things which are not seen are eternal.

II Corinthians 4:18c

For we walk by faith, not by sight.

II Corinthians 5:17

Do not lean to what you can see with your outer eyes. Open your spiritual ones instead. This is not suggesting that you be foolish and go walking through a store with your eyes closed saying, "I know if I can see it with natural eyes, I can't get it." Then you proceed with pushing the cart down the aisles and bumping into everyone. Open your natural eyes but don't look with your natural eyes. There is a word called pre-engrossed. Parents more than likely can relate to this. Pre-engrossment has been instilled in you even though you weren't taught it in the educational institutions you attended. It means that things can be going on around you and you don't see or hear them. Here is an anecdote to give clarity: The children can be burning down the house and you don't care. You just keep on doing what you were doing. You say, "Oh, I'll dial 911 because I'm going to finish this book I'm reading." That is pre-engrossed.

God wants you to be pre-engrossed in the spirit. He doesn't want you to close your ears by putting ear plugs in them and go driving down the street and everyone else has stopped at the train tracks. Here you are, a born again believer, saying that the Lord said that we are not supposed to walk by the things that we can hear or see, "so I'm going to keep on driving." You drive around all of those cars waiting for the train, and you go out there on the tracks and get run over. Unfortunately, you did not hear the warning bells. God wants you to hear, but He doesn't want you to hear. You can't be foolish. You must use wisdom. You are not one hundred percent spirit yet. As long as you are on this earth, you must realize that you have a flesh body. You have to use your eyes, ears, taste, touch and smell for things that require usage of the natural senses. The reason that God gave us natural senses is so that we can function properly in our flesh bodies. He does not expect you to live life based on your feelings but based on His Word which is spirit. We must hear what God is saying about us when we need a miracle or a blessing. You must not listen to those who speak words to you that don't line up with God's Word. If you accept the natural things around you and not the things which exist in the spirit world, you will have the sickness, defeat, poverty and fear that you see and hear so much about. Instead of receiving the negative things of life, receive the positive things of the Spirit. The Spirit gives us life more abundantly.

3
Actions

Actions
Belief
Confidence

ACTIONS, based on *BELIEF*, sustained by the *CONFIDENCE*, that whatever God has said, He will do.

But without faith it is impossible to please him; for he that cometh to God must believe that he is, and that he is a rewarder of them that diligently seek him.

Hebrews 11:6

In the analysis of the first part of Hebrews 11:6, we can determine the necessity of faith in relation to our "pleasing him" or pleasing God. It states that without faith (pistis; Greek), it is *impossible* to please him. Our desire to please him is an expression of the love that we have for our God and Creator. Faith is belief, first of all, in the existence of the true and living God. Without this belief, it cannot be said that God exists because you have not seen a visible, physical image of Him. By the utilization of faith, we iterate that God does truly exist. We can't base His state of being upon the edifices, buildings, or housings that we call the temple of God. There is no visible proof of Him inhabiting a structure, although we refer to the places where we worship as the place where God dwells. He dwells in us and He comes into the house of worship and praise when the people of God (a chosen generation, a royal priesthood, a holy nation, a peculiar people) are assembled together. Therefore we say in accordance that "this is His house." God loves it when He hears our confession of faith declaring that He does indeed exist. We then exhibit evidence of our ability to leave the realm of the senses, intellect and carnality. This is pertinent to walking in the realm of the spirit.

If we believe God does exist, we can also believe that God will reward us if we diligently seek Him. There is something in this portion of the verse (Hebrews 11:6) that is very important. It does not say that God will reward us if we seek after things. This is an area in which many believers impose detriment upon their success and their receiving from the Lord in this life. Their thoughts are consumed with seeking after various things. The Word of God specifically states to diligently seek Him. If your main focus is on seeking after things, that leaves minimal time to seek God and develop an intimacy with Him. When the people of God seek Him, He will add the things you need unto you:

But seek ye first the kingdom of God, and his righteousness; and all these things shall be added unto you.
                                                    Matthew 6:33

Actions 23

We must understand that God wants all of our time. He's a jealous God. Under the law or under grace, He is yet a jealous God. He becomes jealous when you give anything or anyone too much time. He acknowledges that there are things that you must tend to and places that you must go. He knows that you can and expects you to give Him quality time. When He doesn't get it, He will allow the enemy (satan) to implement and afflict you with tests and trials that cause havoc in your life. God wants you to come to the evident realization that He must be first and foremost. He will then rebuke the "evil one" from your life. The amount of time that you will have to endure chastisement and scourging depends upon how long it takes you to turn your attention to the Father. For instance, if you ever had a mate or someone who wanted attention from you, you are familiar with some of the tactics and maneuvers they used in order to get that attention. They would use certain gestures and make all kinds of distracting sounds and noises. You finally grant them an audience and you discover all that your mate or friend wanted was some of your time. After you have responded accordingly, they do great and loving things for you. It's the same with God. Seek God and He will give you the desires of your heart. It is plain and simple.

In the past, I erroneously acted in faith. I thought that faith was seeking things and acting upon that which I thought (I emphasize thought) was expected of me by God. I became enlightened by reading Mark 11:23-24.

For verily I say unto you, That whosoever shall say unto this mountain, Be thou removed, and be thou cast into the sea; and shall not doubt in his heart, but shall believe that those things which he saith shall come to pass; he shall have whatsoever he saith.

Mark 11:23

Therefore I say unto you, What things soever ye desire, when ye pray believe that ye receive them, and ye shall have them.

Mark 11:24

I learned that God wanted me to say to the mountain "get out of the way". He wanted me to do it based upon my relationship with Him. It would be useless for me to utter a command and expect to get the results I'm looking for if my relationship with the Lord is not up to par. It would violate the principle that applies to the situation with the seven sons of Sceva:

And there were seven sons of one Sceva a Jew, and chief of the priests, which did so.

Acts 19:14

And the evil spirit answered and said, Jesus I know, and Paul I know: but who are ye?

Acts 19:15

And the man in whom the evil spirit was leaped on them, and overcame them, and prevailed against them so that they fled out of that house naked and wounded.

Acts 19:16

They attempted to cast the demon out of a man. They were not built up in the Lord. The demon empowered the man. He attacked them and tore their clothes off. They fled out of the house naked and wounded. They didn't have a perfect relationship with God. They had been following the Christians around while observing them. They also knew about Paul the apostle. As a matter of fact, they charged the demon to come out in the name of Jesus by whom Paul preached. The evil spirit said, "Jesus I know, Paul I know, but who are you?" Demons don't recognize your facial features. They recognize your knowledge of the Word of God and the application of its spiritual truths. They recognize the closeness, (intimacy) and dedication that you have to God. You can shout Jesus, Jesus, Jesus all that you want, if you are not built up in the Word of God, the devils are not going to tremble. When you fortify yourself by praying in the spirit, praying on your most holy faith, the devils will identify you when you are in their presence. That is the reason why some believers can operate in the realm of the spirit more fluently than others. These believers are devoted to spending an ample amount of time in prayer and fasting. God said that He will give the gifts to every man severally as He will:

> *Now there are diversities of gifts, but the same Spirit.*
> I Corinthians 12:4

> *But all these worketh that one and the selfsame Spirit, dividing to every man severally as he will.*
> I Corinthians 12:11

> *God also bearing them witness, both with signs and wonders, and with divers miracles, and gifts of the Holy Ghost, according to his own will?*
> Hebrews 2:4

God will also give gifts to them that are readily available for servitude in obedience to Him. If there is blockage, interference or distraction, you're not going to be able to operate in the gifts of the spirit. It doesn't make any difference how many gifts you profess to have. You will find that the gifts that God so frequently manifested through you will be nullified if you're not walking in line with God's Word.

The Word of God says that He will reward us for diligently seeking him. We have assurance that whatever doors that have been closed because of doubt, sickness or unbelief will fly open. God will administer to you all of the spiritual blessings that He has already provided for us in the heavenly places:

Blessed be the God and Father of our Lord Jesus Christ, who hath blessed us with all spiritual blessings in heavenly places in Christ.

Ephesians 1:3

You must establish a close and deeply personal relationship with Him. It gives God great pleasure to reward you because of your steadfastness. Rewarding or blessing is an intrinsic part of God's character.

For we walk by faith, not by sight.

II Corinthians 5:7

How would a person be able to walk without moving? It cannot be done. It requires specific movements or actions for walking. This verse of scripture is saying that we take action by belief.

So then faith cometh by hearing, and hearing by the Word of God.

Romans 10:17

Our faith is developed and erected by a continual hearing of the Word of God. We walk or live by what is written in the scriptures. "Well, Brother Singleton, I agree with that to a certain extent, but I believe that we must exercise common sense." Yes, you exercise common sense, but you must exercise faith more so than common sense. Faith replaces common sense because reliance on it will not get you healed or make you prosperous. To be ruled solely by common sense is for those who are common. We are an uncommon people. We are a chosen generation, a royal priesthood, a holy nation. We're peculiar people that should show forth the praises of him who has called us out of darkness into his marvelous light (I Peter 2:9). Common sense deals with darkness. The moment that Adam committed high treason and sold out our right standing to the enemy, satan became the god of this world. This atmosphere was seized by the power of darkness. He is the power of darkness and there is no light in him. He is the god of this world and the world is a direct reflection of the wickedness, corruption, and evil that is contained in him.

As long as your actions are governed by your senses; how you feel, what people say to you, what you can taste, what you can touch and see, you will be defeated in this life. When will believers learn to act upon the Word of God? Many have acted haphazardly on the words and advice of friends, relatives, and even people that they don't know. Some people believe whatever is told to them by their employers or doctors or whatever the news media has reported. Why don't Christians believe that which is entailed in God's Word? It is our encyclopedia for successful living and the author is the Almighty God.

The Entity Of Two Worlds
And The Activity Of Life Therein

There is another world running concurrent with this earth realm. Let us deal with that one first seeing that it was first in existence.

The first realm is the spirit realm. This is the realm in which a person enters into upon receiving his born again experience. The spirit realm is the locality where God is and He lives in the part called the third heaven, which is in its entirety, His kingdom. God's throne is situated in the most pre-eminent, palatial mansion of the greatest magnitude in beauty and splendor of which we must stand in awe. Mere words in the languages of man cannot describe that which is far above because it escapes the finest, most reverent words contained in the human intellect. It consists of all other inhabitants including the angels, seraphims (Isaiah 6:2), creatures (Ezekiel 1), beasts (Revelation 4:6-9) four and twenty elders (Revelation 4:4). It also consists of those things that are not yet known to man. It is far beyond the capacity and abilities of the finite mind to comprehend:

> *But as it is written, Eye hath not seen, nor ear heard, neither have entered into the heart of man, the things which God hath prepared for them that love him.*
>
> I Corinthians 2:9

A lower section of the heavenlies provides residence for more inhabitants of the spirit realm: satan, principalities, powers, rulers of the darkness of this world, spiritual wickedness in high places:

> *For we wrestle not against flesh and blood, but against principalities, against powers, against the rulers of the darkness of this world, against spiritual wickedness in high places.*
>
> Ephesians 6:12

The spirit realm consists of the unseen or invisible life.

The second realm is the three-dimensional earth realm. It consists of all of the things that are seen surrounding you and the things that are afar off, even the things that are microscopic and telescopic.

If something is dimensional, it is described as having a measurable extent such as depth, breadth, length, or thickness. God is eternal and omnipresent. He therefore can and does exist in one dimension of time and space and co-exist in another because all time and space is contained within Him. He sits in one dimension and rest His feet in another:

> *Thus saith the Lord, The heaven is my throne, and the earth is my footstool: where is the house that ye build me? and where is the place of my rest?*
>
> Isaiah 66:1

Through our rebirth experience, we have access to both the spiritual world and the three-dimensional earth realm. We are down here on the earth but through our recreated spirits, our prayers, petitions, supplications, praises and worship reach up to the third heaven (God's throne).

Spiritual Blessings: Overstocked And Often Unclaimed

Blessed be the God and Father of our Lord Jesus Christ, who hath blessed us with all spiritual blessings in heavenly places in Christ.

Ephesians 1:3

The moment a person believes the gospel of Jesus Christ, they are saved. They become reborn on the inside. The inner man has been recreated by believing in the heart that Jesus is Lord and God has raised him from the dead. If a person doesn't make one move on the outside, it has no bearing on his or her new birth. God gives us so much grace in this age that if a person would prefer to die of illness or disease rather than expire after a long, full life spent in good health, God would allow it without any intervention on His behalf. It is His will that everyone be healed, but He is not going to heal anyone by using force. His grace is sufficient enough for a person to lie on a sick bed and shout their way to glory if that's what he or she desires. If a person wants to be healed, His grace is sufficient for that also.

Some believers read Ephesians 1:3 and insert material blessings for an interpretation that is more pleasing to them. It does not say material blessings. It asserts spiritual blessings. The reason it says spiritual blessings is because the things that we need or desire exist firstly in the spirit world. God is a spirit and we must communicate spiritual things by the Spirit. In order to reap the benefits of having all the spiritual blessings, we must first believe that they are inside of us. We must know that they are part of our inheritance that can be transferred from the realm of the spirit by faith into the three-dimensional earth realm. When you receive this into your heart, God will give you the power to successfully achieve spiritually and naturally.

In order for your outer man to receive the same benefits of the spirit world, you will have to act on the Word of God outwardly. Your acting on the promises of God inwardly resulted in you being born again. Believing God's Word did not require you to use any physical human effort whatsoever. Your believing and acceptance of His Word was brought on by the mental and spiritual convictions you displayed. When you confessed with your mouth what was conceived in your heart, that required physical human effort. Confession is the end result of believing. Because you get all of the blessings of God by believing in your heart, you have received healings, finances, etc. in the spirit. You cannot have the manifestations of those things until your actions correspond with your belief or faith. As your actions directly relate to what you believe, you will obtain that same confidence outwardly that is embedded in your heart. Most Christians can say without hesitation "we walk by faith and not by sight." The problems arise when it is time to get those feet moving and those hands working after our bold confession. Don't say that you believe and remain dormant! The devil doesn't want you to act on the Word of God. He'll tell you that faith doesn't require action. Your actions based on belief conveys that you actually trust in this God whom you have praised so highly. You must say, "I believe it, I receive it, I am acting on it. I am walking by faith and that's it. I have no more excuses. I am not hesitating anymore. This is for me and I'm going to get it all!" Don't be troubled by the circumstances that bombard you. Concentrating on the immediate circumstances that confront you can cause you to develop a defeatist attitude.

The Word of God says in I Peter 2:4 that Christ bore our sins in his own body on the tree...by whose stripes ye were healed. You must believe this firstly if you're seeking healing from God. Apply the actions that directly correlate with that which you are "faithing" for. For example, if you couldn't move your right arm, you say, "I'm going to move this arm. I believe that in accordance with God's Word." You attempt to move your arm and after several or maybe one attempt you can move it. You're going to start waving it and shouting, "Glory!" It was not until the woman with the issue of blood touched the Lord and then she was healed. She acted on what she believed and said, "If I can but touch the hem of his garment." She pressed her way through the crowd to reach Jesus. When the Lord asked who touched him, she confessed that it was her. She believed, confessed and then acted on her heartfelt confession.

Actions Consequently Bring Relief To Financial Anxieties

Several believers say that they need a "financial miracle." The first thing that you must know is that finances will be given to you by God channeling it through man. God will use man as an employer, benefactor, or perhaps a mate to supply you with some form of income. You must be accepting of the methods and people which God will use. His Word plainly states that if you give it shall be given unto you. How? Man shall give unto your bosom (Luke 6:38). The Lord is not going to rain money from the sky for you. If you say that the

Lord is going to send you a financial blessing, act on what you believe. God may open up a door for you to get a job or a prolific career opportunity. Employment produces a steady flow of income, not just a one-time incident, such as a settlement, an unexpected check in the mail, recompense for a loan, etc. If you are seeking to be gainfully employed, be specific about the kind of job that you want.

Most people have been taught to tithe and you will receive blessings. If you have sown a seed, that indicates that you had input. You allocated funds to be used for the kingdom of God. How are you going to get a return on that which you have given in faith? You must have access to designated financial resources. Again I say it will be through man, which more than likely is going to be an employer. Some believers want to get financial miracles because of the absence of drive and ambition, laxity in working habits, or just sheer laziness. Stop thinking that you will get something for nothing.

God taught wisdom through his apostles. Unfortunately, there is not enough being taught on this subject matter. If you are not told these things, you might sit idly around with the expectation that God is going to do everything. You might even believe that you don't have to lift a finger at anytime because you say "God will provide." You say, "I'm going to get a new house." If you don't get out there and select the house of your choice, you're not going to be the owner of a new house. Perhaps, someone wants to give you a house. How would this determine this if you don't let the fact be known that you want one, unless God miraculously reveals it to them. You should not be seeking miracles all of the time. You must use wisdom in most cases:

If any of you lack wisdom, let him ask of God, that giveth to all men liberally, and upbraideth not; and it shall be given him.

James 1:5

You could say, "I believe that God shall supply all of my need. (Philippians 4:19) I need a house. Father, will you give me a job that pays enough money that I will be able to put a down payment on the house in six months?" All of a sudden, because of your faithfulness in tithing, the door opens and God blesses you with a job out of nowhere. You have a position as something that the devil said you could never be. You may now take the money that God has blessed you with and put it down on the house you want. The next thing is to trust God for the mortgage payments. You are faithfully paying your bills and continuing to faithfully tithe. God will bless you with increases in your salary so that you can get a bigger and better house in a more upscale neighborhood:

His lord said unto him, Well done, thou good and faithful servant: thou has been faithful over a few things, I will make thee ruler over many things: enter thou into the joy of the lord.

Matthew 25:21

If you find yourself at a point in life where there are many doors open for you, you can choose the one that you want. If there is only one door open, walk through it. It might lead to another door that has behind it your heart's desire.

Now when he had left speaking, he said unto Simon, Launch out into the deep, and let down your nets for a draught. And Simon answering said unto him, Master, we have toiled all the night, and have taken nothing: nevertheless at thy word I will let down the net. And when they had this done, they inclosed a great multitude of fishes: and their net brake. And they beckoned unto their partners, which were in the other ship, that they should come and help them. And they came, and filled both the ships, so that they began to sink.

Luke 5:4-7

Jesus told Peter to cast his net into the sea one more time, even though he had been toiling all night and hadn't caught any fish. Peter might have been hesitant and wondering why. After all, he felt that he had given it a sufficient amount of time. He then said, "nevertheless, at thy word I will let down the net." Peter did as he was instructed to do by Jesus and that was when he was blessed. "At thy word," the Word of the Almighty God, is what we base our belief upon. His word is sure, faithful and true, always bringing forth the results that are promised by Him. The Word of God says, with the stripes of Jesus we are healed; but my God shall supply all of your need according to his riches in glory by Christ Jesus; if you believe you shall be saved. These are all covenant promises. Now, that you are made aware of them, receive them for yourself and act on them.

Financial problems and their related frustrations are one of the main adversities plaguing believers today. You have to realize that what you have on the inside didn't require money to obtain. God didn't stipulate in the scriptures that you have to have great wealth before you can be saved. Salvation is free and is given by grace through faith. God recreates you on the inside just by you believing that Jesus Christ went to the cross, went to hell, rose again and justified you. Do you want to see the effects of your salvation on the outside? I reiterate—ACT ON YOUR BELIEF!

4
Belief

Denominationalism And Its Effect On Believing God's Word

Most people tend to have a belief in one thing or another. This is an area in which many Christians have failed and they cannot receive the things of God. God doesn't want us to merely have a belief. He wants us to have full confidence and trust in His Word.

Many affiliated churches have denominational beliefs. Denominationalism governs the lives of those who have made a commitment to its organizations. Denominations have an organizational structure and they have certain criteria they want and expect you to adhere to. They specify believing in this and denouncing that. Their beliefs and disbeliefs are based upon the things their hierarchy has deemed to be truth: (meeting their standards of approval) or contrary, radical, unethical, or passé (not their cup of tea). Some of their rules and regulations might not necessarily line up with the Word of God because they are founded of man's interpretation instead of being the unadulterated revelation given by the Holy Spirit. Faith is not just what you believe or what someone has told you to believe. Faith is what you believe based upon that which you hear from God. If the Word doesn't say it, then it should not be your belief.

Denominationalism promotes separatism and often causes disharmony within the body of Christ. Some denominational beliefs overshadow the teachings established by Jesus during his time here on earth. Christ redeemed us from the curse of the law, for the letter killeth. Some denominations have not received this and have bound believers with burdensome works that coincide with their beliefs. There are denominations that feel they have a monopoly on salvation. Believers never come into the depth and fullness of their relationship with the Lord because the hierarchy keeps them ignorant of God's will. Some denominations denounce the baptism of the Holy Spirit. Speaking in tongues (heavenly utterance) is among the great controversies. If there is one Lord, one faith, one baptism, why is it that things such as speaking in tongues, (which should be characteristic of believers), prophecy, and spiritual gifts such as word of knowledge and the other gifts have such negative connotations put on them? Why would God give spiritual gifts to believers affiliated with one denomination or no denomination and not to all believers if we are supposed to be members of one body? He is not a respecter of persons. If you don't believe in something, God is not going to force it on you. Tongues can and will cross denominational lines if you allow it to and receive it by faith. Why deny yourself of something that should be intrinsic and inherent among believers? Satan's job is to keep believers weak, powerless, and forever lukewarm. Why rob yourself and rob God of the opportunity to fortify and mold His people in the way that He chooses because He knows what is most profitable for believers? We limit God so very often when He wants to prove himself strong and incomparable in our lives.

Most recently God tore down the walls of separatism and bondage resulting from communism in some foreign countries. The wall coming down and changes in governmental rule were not accomplished solely through the efforts of man, but God was in the forefront of these occurrences. This was accomplished so that prophecies may be fulfilled. The gospel must be preached to all nations. He has opened the doors, but he doesn't want the new converts to be ensnared by denominationalism. He wants them to receive the truth taught by those who are used by the Spirit of Truth. Jesus is coming soon. There is no time, nor should there be any tolerance for yokes of bondage brought on by religion and traditions of man. You must examine your beliefs. Are they truly founded on the principles and precepts in God's Word (His Word being spirit and life) or are they fleshly or carnal, pleasing man in his own thinking and feeding his pride? Satan is the culprit behind the separatism initiated by denominationalism. Those who are given to religiosity have let themselves be used of the enemy by receiving the imaginations and high things that have exalted themselves against the knowledge of God:

> *Casting down imaginations, and every high thing that exalteth itself against the knowledge of God, and*

bringing into captivity every thought to the obedience of Christ.

II Corinthians 10:5

The Fall Of A Chosen People

If there is something in the Word that is not written to you, although it is in the Word, it is *not* meant for you. There is more than one person's mail in the scriptures. There is Israel's mail and there is the Gentiles' mail. There is prophecy and there is gospel.

Israel was a special people that God had ordained to be his own. They displeased God because of their lack of belief. God, in turn, chose another group of people to provoke Israel to jealousy, who are referred to as Gentiles. He wrote certain things that were solely intended for Israel. They were not designed in purpose for the Gentiles. Why? God was dealing with Israel as a special people. He made them inheritors of an abundance of blessings and favor. They were the recipients of His most prized and divine love. After several occasions of Him forgiving them for their transgressions and lack of trust, God had determined that Israel was not going to obey Him. They had numerous counts of repetitive disobedient acts against them. He then allowed a curse to befall them. God did not place the curse of the law upon the Gentiles. Paul wrote that the Gentiles did not have the law:

For when the Gentiles, which have not the law, do by nature the things contained in the law, these, having not the law, are a law unto themselves.

Romans 2:14

Gentiles were classified as heathens. The term "gentile" defined actually means heathen. The Bible says that the Gentiles were strangers and foreigners from God's promises and covenants. God took the Gentiles and engrafted them into His family. Why? This was done as a means of provoking the Jewish man into emulation or unto jealousy. Because God initiated that, we can be the recipients of all of the promises that He made to Israel. I am referring to the good promises. We don't have to take hold of the curses.

A Call To Duty For The Gentiles

I say then, Have they stumbled that they should fall? God forbid: but rather through their fall salvation is come unto the Gentiles, for to provoke them to jealousy.

Romans 11:11

We are to understand that God is using the Gentiles to provoke the Jewish man to jealousy. If we are being used to provoke him to jealousy, we must have something to provoke him to jealousy with. The Jewish man did not receive the salvation of Christ because they didn't receive Jesus as the Messiah. They're still waiting for the Messiah although He has already come. God gave him to us (Gentiles) because the Word of God says whosoever believes in the Lord shall be saved:

For God so loved the world that he gave his only begotten Son, that whosoever believeth in him should not perish, but have everlasting life.

John 3:16

Salvation is not only to the Jew, but to every man. God has given us this salvation. The Jews became jealous because they knew that previously the Gentile was nothing in the eyesight of God. They knew that the Gentile was uncared for. We know now that God cares for us, and we are also heirs to the kingdom and the great and precious promises of God. This was God using psychology. He took a nation of people who were unloved and undesirable and gave to them life and love.

God sent the Apostle Paul to preach the message of Jesus to the Gentile as part of his plan to incite the Jewish man into a jealous state due to being displaced by a dishonorable nation of people. Parents who adore their children will give them whatever they desire as long as it is not harmful to them. If parents have a favorite child and that child becomes disobedient, they turn their love, affection and praise to one of their other children. Even though this child was desired less, he would obey and do the things which pleased his parents. The child who once had all of the favor will realize that the other sibling now has the things he once had and will choose to give his rebellion because he has been made jealous.

Israel, who had been incomparable and second to none in the eyesight of God, was now being rivaled in affection and favor. Today the Jewish man is yet being made jealous of the salvation in which the Gentile has embraced and is blossoming in. Individuals become jealous of others if a person has more than they have or if someone is gaining on them; if you are intervening in something that they had a monopoly on; if you are as talented or more talented and stealing the spotlight, the applause, the praise; or if someone is as beautiful or more beautiful than they. No one likes to give up first place.

For I speak to you Gentiles, inasmuch as I am the apostle of the Gentiles, I magnify mine office: If by any means I may provoke to emulation them which are my flesh, and might save some of them. For if the casting away of them be the reconciling of the world, what shall the receiving of them be, but life from the dead?

Romans 11:13-15

The reconciliation of the world was wrought on the "casting away of the Jewish nation." It granted opportunity for every man to walk uninhibited into God's presence. The Gentiles are now entitled to all of the things that had previously belonged to the Jewish people. If we, by our great prosperity and accomplishments through the favor of God, fulfill the part we are to portray as Gentiles in successfully provoking the Jewish man to jealousy, the blessings of the Lord will eventually overtake us. Believers today feel that they are blessed because they have received things from God such as a house, car, mate, etc. They are contented with the involvements of their own little world after receiving their salvation. Salvation is not given to us so that we can enjoy its material benefits alone. We are also to be light to all unbelievers and those "of little faith." If a Jewish person comes to believe in Jesus because of your favor from God and manifestations of it, it is compared to being brought from death unto life. The subject of provoking the Jewish man to jealousy is never really a topic for teaching or discussion. Why is this "taboo" among the members of the five-fold ministry? It is scripture and should be instilled in the minds of believers. It is not to be taught so that we may be lifted up in pride because we are "receiving the spoil" so to speak. We are not to boast or feel that we are superior to our Jewish brothers because they have not yet come into full knowledge of the truth concerning Jesus. For it has not been by our works of righteousness that we have been blessed with salvation, but it is by the grace of the true and living God. The Word of God says, "have they stumbled that they should fall? God forbid." They have not fallen to be cast away irrevocably but to be brought unto subjection and be illuminated to see the error they made in discerning spiritual truth. If we are successful in our walk with the Lord, the Jewish people will notice and realize that Addonai has given all of the things that once belonged solely to them, to the Gentiles. The Gentiles have salvation, great wealth, healing and miracles. Israel will ponder over this and in humility they will believe. They will believe in the Jesus of Nazareth that walked among the their ancestors over 2,000 years ago and desire the salvation that he was made a ransom for; that he became the sacrificial lamb of God for. They will believe he loves them and that he always has and always will. Are you, as a Gentile, accomplishing the missions that you were engrafted into the family of God for?

The Measure Of Faith

For I say, through the grace given unto me, to every man that is among you, not to think of himself more highly than he ought to think; but to think soberly, according as God hath dealt to every man the measure of faith.

Romans 12:3

Some believers might have thought that when they became born again, they had an elevated level of faith.

This is not true. All of mankind has received the measure of faith (a portion of faith). The measure denotes a specific amount, which actually is the least amount of faith that we can have. God planted a seed of faith in you at the time of your conception, in expectation that the seed would procreate unto maturation. If God had not implanted the measure of faith in you, you could reject the Word, because it had no foundation or basis on which it could develop. Therefore, He could not contest your refusal to accept His Word. We are given the measure of faith so that when God's Word is ministered to us, we can believe it. The Word of God is not so far-fetched, so abstract, so insane that we cannot accept it as being true.

Mix And Measure

Let us therefore fear, lest, a promise being left us of entering into his rest, any of you should seem to come short of it. For unto us was the gospel preached, as well as unto them: but the word preached did not profit them, not being mixed with faith in them that heard it.
Hebrews 4:1-2

How can you mix something if there are not two or more elements?

In order to have a mixture, constituent parts are combined or blended together. If the measure of faith and Word of God are mixed together, the seed of faith begins to grow. A person is stagnant until he or she hears the truth of God. The moment that a person hears the raw gospel, something happens. It doesn't matter who they are or what walk of life they are from. Society or family background is no hindrance to the Word of God. When the Word of God is taught, people believe it and their faith gradually or rapidly increases depending on how receptive an individual is.

There are no exceptions to the rule regarding every man having the measure of faith. Although mankind has those who don't display it. It does not mean that the measure of faith is not in existence in them. This also includes those who consider themselves as an atheist or agnostic. They have rejected the existence of God out of being foolishly duped by satan:

The fool hath said in his heart, There is no God. They are corrupt, they have done abominable works, there is none that doeth good.

Psalms 14:1

But if our gospel be hid, it is hid to them that are lost: In whom the god of this world hath blinded the minds of them which believe not, lest the light of the glorious gospel of Christ, who is the image of God, should shine unto them.

II Corinthians 4:3-4

Our minds might initially reject the Word but it is the heart (spirit) of man that believes:

For with the heart man believeth unto righteousness; and with the mouth confession is made unto salvation.

Romans 10:10

Our faith is developed over and above the "measure" the more we hear and believe the Word of God. God would have been trying to no avail to get you to receive

His Word if He didn't prime you to receive it. You had to be primed in order for you to even want to come into a building to hear the gospel being preached and taught. He had to put a desire in you to want to know your Creator. Every man has a desire, hunger and need to know his Creator. That is the measure of faith in utilization. If you are instructed by an anointed teacher, the measure of faith mixes with the Word of God and you accrue a mature and solid faith. You must be in a fellowship where you are constantly saturated with the Word of God. The more faith that you receive, the more you have and can act upon. People cannot act on the Word because they lack faith over and above the measure. The measure or primary faith that God starts you off with is not enough to carry you through the tasks we must endure in this life.

God ministered to Israel the same good news that we're blessed by today. They did not mix what was preached to them with the faith contained in them. They formed barriers of unbelief and let the prophecies come to nought in their lives. If they would have taken hold of the Word of God and let it mix, it would have grown and multiplied.

You have a free will to accept or reject the Word. I strongly urge you to mix what is contained in this teaching with the faith that is already in you. If you don't take heed, you will prohibit the growth and development of a higher level of faith.

The Word Yielding Forth Fruit

The sower soweth the word. And these are they by the way-side, where the word is sown; but when they have heard, satan cometh immediately, and taketh away the word that was sown in their hearts.

Mark 4:14-15

The only way that satan can steal something from a born again believer is by that believer rejecting the Word. They heard the Word being taught but didn't believe what was said. Therefore, a believer actually freely hands over his possession of the Word to the devil. Satan gladly snatches it and gloats in his victory. He knows that the Word will give you power over him. There are two ways that you can take something. Something can be taken by force or taken by receiving it. The Bible states not to give him place:

Neither give place to the devil.

Ephesians 4:27

We grant him opportunity to take from us if we give him place. A way-side believer is residing in the area of doubt. They reject the Word immediately. NO WORD— NO FRUIT!! NO PLANTING OF SEEDS, NO HARVESTING OF CROPS!!

And these are they likewise which are sown on stony ground; who, when they have heard the word, immediately receive it with gladness; And have no root in themselves, and so endure but for a time: afterward, when affliction or persecution, ariseth for the word's sake, immediately they are offended.

Mark 4:16-17

These verses of scripture pertain to those believers who receive the word and get excited about it. They jump, they dance, they shout, they run all over the church building and while speaking in tongues, they come riding in on two Hondas. They swing from the lights and anything else that they can get their hands on. The benefits and blessings come because they did believe and accept the Word but they didn't cleave to it long enough to endure the tests and trials. The devil is standing there, taking it all in and planning his next strategy. He waits for the opportune time to pounce. He knows that these individuals did receive the Word when they heard it. When the enemy enacts his persecutions and afflictions upon them, they throw in the towel giving in to defeat. You should know that persecutions and afflictions arise because of the Word. This is the devil using devices to keep you ignorant of God's will. The devil will try to the utmost to put sickness and disease on you. He will try to kill you. The Word of God did not say that we would be sick. It did say that afflictions and persecutions would definitely arise. The devil starts working through your mate, through your children and through your employer. After a season, the "stony ground" believer doubts the Word of God. Your response to satan should be, "Devil, take your junk back because I don't want it and I'm not accepting it!" These believers bear fruit about thirty-fold.

And these are they which are sown among thorns; such as hear the word, And the cares of the world, and the deceitfulness of riches, and the lust of other things entering in, choke the word, and it becometh unfruitful.
Mark 4:18-19

These believers are the ones that received the Word and kept it for a longer period of time than those that endured for a short season. They let the deceitfulness of riches and lust of other things distract them. Lust is often associated with the burning desires of the flesh. You can also lust after material things. Many people in the body of Christ blow it because they are not contented with what they have. They are overtaken in their own greed and covetousness. They have received the Word of God but choose not to prioritize things in their lives. They prefer to make money by working an exorbitant amount of hours on their jobs rather than taking out time to hear the Word of God. There are believers who are wrapped in their various functions and socializations. There are those who are wallowing in their self-pity, burdens and fears. They often say, "I don't feel like going to church today." Some Christians are so busy climbing the ladder of success that they don't have time to look back. These are the believers that bring forth fruit about sixty-fold.

And these are they which are sown on good ground; such as hear the word, and receive it, and bring forth fruit, some thirty-fold, some sixty, and some an hundred.

Mark 4:20

If believers receive the Word wholeheartedly, clinging to it, not doubting but applying it to their lives by faith, they will bring forth fruit at the rate of one hundred-fold. The one hundred-fold believers endure until the end and are not moved by tests and trials. Their eyes are always looking to Jesus. They have perfect peace because their minds are on him. Each believer is capable of bearing fruit one hundred-fold. It is entirely up to you what your relationship with the Lord will be like. Are you dedicated? Is Jesus Christ your all in all? Are you steadfast and unmovable?

Believing Is Receiving

For verily I say unto you, that whosoever shall say unto this mountain, Be thou removed, and be thou cast into the sea; and shall not doubt in his heart, but shall believe that those things which he saith shall come to pass; he shall have whatsoever he saith. Therefore I say unto you, What things soever ye desire, when ye pray, believe that ye receive them, and ye shall have them.

Mark 11:23-24

How can you believe you shall receive the things you pray for? You must develop your faith. Developing faith requires specific procedures that you must follow which advances us to each stage of growth and development. These procedures necessitate hearing the Word of God and believing in your heart what the Word says. Constant exposure to the gospel of Jesus Christ builds our faith, preparing us for the undertaking of Christian life. We must hear the Word so that we will know how to pray according to God's will. We will be able to speak to the mountains in our lives and know they will heed to our commands because we speak the word of faith.

5

Confidence

For we are made partakers of Christ, if we hold the beginning of our confidence steadfast unto the end;
                                        Hebrews 3:14

I often say that, "I have everything that Christ has. Jesus is seated in heavenly places. I am there also":

And hath raised us up together, and made us sit together in heavenly places in Christ Jesus:
                                        Ephesians 2:6

"One day, I will take on a new glorified body and it will be joined together with my inner man when Jesus comes. He will rapture the church and we will go up to glory." The aforementioned statements are true indeed but there is a prerequisite that must not be overlooked. It states, "if we hold the beginning of our confidence steadfastly until the end." People say, "I know I'm saved." "How do you know that you are saved?" it is asked. "I'm saved because I gave up my sinful ways. I gave up fornication. I stopped gambling." You might have based your salvation on these things, but true salvation is based upon you being made a partaker with Christ until He comes. Salvation cannot be centered upon the things of the flesh that you have received deliverance from. Because of the weaknesses contained in the flesh of man, you might succumb and find yourself doing these things once again. Would your salvation be nullified because of your human frailties? If you were believing wholeheartedly that you were saved yesterday, how can it be that you are not saved today? If you are saved, then *YOU ARE SAVED*!! Some believers have mistakenly based their salvation upon things they have given up in the natural due to ignorance. You can have sanctification on the outside because of what you have ceased from, but you cannot base the inward sanctification upon what you have given up. By giving up things outwardly, you are presenting your body as a living sacrifice:

> *I beseech you therefore brethren, by the mercies of God that ye present your bodies a living sacrifice.*
> Romans 12:1a

An outward transformation stems from a change that has occurred firstly on the inside. The change is brought on by hearing the Word of God. Preachers are trying to get the world saved by telling men and women about the way they dress, the way they choose to style their hair and other qualities relating to the outer appearance. Will giving up these things save a person? There are people who have never indulged in some of the things believers say that they have given up. Are they saved because they have not done these things? If a man holds steadfastly to the Word or confidence in Christ until he comes, the Lord has guaranteed you salvation. If you cannot trust in what is written in John 3:16, you cannot trust in what God's Word says as a whole:

For God so loved the world, that he gave his only begotten Son, that whosoever believeth in him should not perish, but have everlasting life.

John 3:16

If you can't believe that, if there are fifty thousand other things contingent upon salvation, there is something wrong with the Word. That verse of scripture is so precise until there is no adding or taking away from it. God so loved the world. There are all kinds of people in the world. There are liars, thieves, and homosexuals. There are people who indulge in diverse kinds of corruption and lasciviousness. Why would God give Christ as a ransom for the sins of man if a person can become righteous enough that he could save himself? Man has gotten the notion that he can "get himself righteous" regardless as to what anyone says or thinks. If achieving righteousness could be accomplished by a man's endeavors, he should have come along about two thousand years ago. He should have proved to God that there was a man on earth that could have been righteous without His Son. God's efforts to find a man to save mankind could have been aborted. God told Isaiah that he was sending a Messiah. Isaiah was not afforded the privilege of seeing the Messiah he prophesied about.

But the scripture hath concluded all under sin, that the promise by faith of Jesus Christ might be given to them that believe.

Galatians 3:22

This scripture verifies the fact that all men were under sin. That was everyone that came before the death of Jesus. In the mind of God, every man that came forth through the bloodline of Adam was under sin. The Bible says that you did not commit any transgressions after the similitude of Adam, but because of what Adam did, all were pronounced sinners:

> *Nevertheless death reigned from Adam to Moses, even over them that had not sinned after the similitude of Adam's transgression, who is the figure of him that was to come.*
>
> Romans 5:14
>
> *Wherefore as by one man sin entered into the world, and death by sin; and so death passed upon all men, for that all have sinned:*
>
> Romans 5:12

A person is not a sinner because of the habits that he or she has. In ignorance, you are a participant in the habit-forming behavior that you possess. If you start something, you have the ability to stop doing that same thing. It doesn't mean because you start and stop doing various things on the outside that the inside has been affected. God doesn't make you a new creature because you relinquish certain things. If He did, don't you think that He would have selected Melchizedek as a candidate for the tasks of being a martyr and sacrifice for the world? He could have spared the life of His precious son Jesus. The Word of God says that Melchizedek didn't have a beginning or ending. It is not known where he originated from:

Without father, without mother, without descent, having neither beginning of days, nor end of life; but made like unto the Son of God; abideth a priest continually.

Hebrews 7:3

There is no documentation indicating where, when or if he died. He could have been translated. God couldn't and didn't use Melchizedek. Why? The reason being that Melchizedek had to continually get his flesh in line. (Your flesh will become disorderly unexpectedly at any moment. You have to fast and pray to keep it under subjection. You will have problems with it as long as your mind is carnal. That is why the Word says to renew your mind daily. It has to be renewed by the Word of God.) God knew that there was not a man worthy to die for mankind. He took the responsibility on himself: The Holy Spirit impregnated Mary and she brought forth a son, Jesus. Jesus, not being born of a relationship between a male and female, but being born of a relationship between the Holy Spirit and that female. Jesus didn't have the same blood of Adam running through his veins, therefore he could not be a sinner. He had to be made a sinner in order to die for all men. God laid the sins of man on Christ and he died for all mankind.

For we have not a high priest which cannot be touched with the feeling of our infirmities; But was in all points tempted like as we are, yet without sin.

Hebrews 4:15

Jesus was tempted in the different areas of his life just as we are today, but he did not commit sin. There was an incident that took place in the temple, involving Jesus and his flesh did become upset. If he had never gotten upset, his reaction to the vendors or merchants who had turned the "house of prayer" into a marketplace, wouldn't have been whipping them out of the temple. The Word of God indicates that "he was yet without sin" because he couldn't sin. Why couldn't he sin? Jesus didn't inherit the sin nature. The fact that you cannot sin if you don't have a sin nature is something that people cannot comprehend. If there is no sin nature, there cannot be any sinful acts perpetrated by an individual. The word sin is derived from the Greek word harmatia, which means error. Jesus couldn't error because he did not have a nature of error in him is another way of saying it. Who could lay a charge against him? He could only be charged with breaking the law of Moses.

The sinful nature of man is not only contained within the walls of his inner state of being but also on the outside of him. We have been redeemed from the sinful nature within us and in correspondence with that, we must bring our hands and feet under subjection. We are partakers of our accession of freedom on the inside, therefore we must seek the equivalent freedom on the outside. We must walk in the spirit so that we will not fulfill the lust of the flesh.

For we are made partakers of Christ, if we hold the beginning of our confidence steadfast unto the end;
                                        Hebrews 3:14

What if a person's beginning of their confidence was not based upon the grace of God? That person would be holding on to something that is futile. He or she thinks they are saved but they're not. They're adhering to a self-salvation, a self-righteousness:

For they being ignorant of God's righteousness, and going about to establish their own righteousness, have not submitted themselves unto the righteousness of God.

Romans 10:3

They're holding on to these things and not to the "beginning of our confidence" that we first received. What is that which we first received? This is the salvation given to us by Jesus Christ:

For by grace are you saved through faith; and that not of yourselves: it is the gift of God: Not of works, lest any man should boast.

Ephesians 2:9

Our confidence should be based upon the Word of God. The word confidence comes from the Greek word hypostasis, which actually means assurance. It also means support and undergirding, a setting under, a guarantee, a pledge, warrant, promise, agreement, covenant, a pact and an understanding. If we cling undyingly to that assurance, we will receive with certainty the manifestations of God's promises. Our salvation is dependent upon our cleaving to that pact which God has made with us. You should absolutely hold to it. Your actions should be based on your belief, sustained by the guarantee. You, in all assuredness, can hold on to the fact that you will receive everything stipulated in the covenant promises of God.

The reason why some believers don't have their needs met outwardly is because they are lacking inwardly. They have not ascertained whether or not they are truly saved. They're running, working, climbing in all effort to achieve perfection, a perfection in which they never quite reach the summit. Their salvation is never brought unto perfection because they equate it with works.

Can you trust God's Word? Do you have a covenant that guarantees blessings outwardly? Do you have a covenant that guarantees you salvation inwardly? If you answered yes to these questions, and have not yet seen the manifestations, simply hold to it. Remember, we are walking by faith and not by sight. We are not hindered by the things that are seen because we know that they are temporal. After their season, they shall surely pass. God has given power through faith to change impossible circumstances. We don't have to be fearful and overcome with doubt:

For God hath not given us the spirit of fear; but of power, and of love, and of a sound mind.

II Timothy 1:7

Our minds and hearts are to be focused in on the ultimate of guarantees, the Word of God.

We are to believe God's Word and act upon it with the understanding that it is our sole support.

But without faith it is impossible to please him; for he that cometh to God must believe that he is, and that he is a rewarder of them that diligently seek him.

Hebrews 11:6

You're diligently seeking the support. You're diligently seeking the covenant. You're diligently seeking the pact. You want to know everything about this guarantee. The more you seek, the more you will find. The more you knock, the more the doors shall open. Remember, God is a rewarder, but you must have confidence in him. You must have confidence in His Word. You have confidence that the actions you take based upon your belief are genuine and believe that they will bring manifestations.

Being confident of this very thing, that he which hath begun a good work in you will perform it until the day of Jesus:

Philippians 1:6

That particular word confident comes from the Greek word *pytho*, which actually means to be convinced, be pacified. You can pacify yourself by trusting implicitly in God's Word, knowing whatever he says, He will do. You could confess, "I know that God has begun a good work in me. I know that He is going to perform it. I know that I am saved, not based upon the things I gave up. My salvation is based upon what God gave up for me." You need to rely on God. Believing, trusting, relying and yielding to God is evidence of the confidence you have in Him. If you have confidence in that work that God has begun in you, He will continue to do that work in you until the coming of Jesus Christ. How much more will you see the results of it if you act upon the work he is perfecting in you?

There are some believers that say, "I've been acting and doing what the Word says, but it's not working." There is some doubt there already. If you spend most of your time looking at the guarantee, you're not going to spend any time worrying about the guarantee not being made good. In other words, you must have assurance that whatever God has said, He will perform.

Being confident of this very thing, that he which hath begun a good work in you will perform it until the day of Jesus Christ:

Philippians 1:6

If Jesus doesn't come for another thousand years, God will perform the good work in you until then. He's not going to let you down. You can bank on God; you can rely on him. Philippians 4:19 says, but my God shall supply all of your need...You have been saying, "My needs are not met." You have just expressed a lack of faith and assurance in the guarantee. Stop doubting the Word of God! Take your actions based on that which you believe from hearing the Word of God. Take your actions based on the hearing of the Word of faith and sustain your actions by assurance. Think about the agreement that God has made every time the devil tells you that something is not going to happen. Think about all that God has specified in the Word for you. Think about how much God has sacrificed so that you may have the desires of your heart.

OUR BOLD CONFESSION:
We Act In Faith Based On That Which We Believe
And Sustain Our Actions By Confidence

The end result is a life of fruitfulness; a life of having all of your needs met and all of your bills paid! You are to begin to act on the Word of God without wavering:

But let him ask in faith, nothing wavering. For he that wavereth is like a wave of the sea driven with the wind and tossed. For let not that man think that he shall receive anything of the Lord.

James 1:7

The blessings that you receive will outweigh the tests and trials that you have endured.

My friends, grab hold of the Word of God with a strong tenacious grip of courage. Refuse to let go. Defy any and every authority that comes against you. Stand on the Word until you watch the Word become manifest in your life. It is always a blessing to be able to see the written Word become the manifested Word.

Remember, your actions based on your present belief, sustained by confidence that whatever God has said he will do: this will bring the blessings of God on the scene. You deserve the blessings of God because He has already said that they are for you. Why not receive them all? Know what is yours and don't give up until you have it in your hand.

6

God Can Be Trusted

In this last chapter, I would like to express to you the importance of God's trustworthiness.

Trustworthiness is something that is earned by an individual because of his actions, reputation, and overall character. Dependability, truthfulness, availability, and accuracy are some of the character traits of a trustworthy person. We will explore each trait to give the full spectrum of what is being implied about trustworthiness.

Dependability   Let's break that word down:
   Depend — Can you rely on a person to follow through on things that he promises? Can you lean on him for support, morally, financially, etc.? Can you need him? In other words, is he important enough to your life to be considered as a need or a means of survival? Is this person reliable enough to

have a prominent position in your life? *Ability* — Is this person capable in strength, knowledge, means, and performance?

Together, these words describe a person who is able to produce results/The results that are needed for a successful outcome.

Availability Are you able to make contact with a person, even on short notice? Will he or she come when you ask them to? Is this person never around when you need him? Will this individual run everytime you mention the word commitment? Do you have to go through several channels to get to this person?

If a person is available, he or she is accessible, willing and ready to do what is asked or required of him or her.

Accuracy You might wonder how accuracy comes into play. Consider this. if a person is not accurate, not precise, not timely, the things that he does for you might not necessarily prove to be beneficial to you. He could make the wrong decisions in life or death situations. He might do too little or too much. He might interfere when you don't need his help or his opinion. He will hinder you in completing things or endeavors that you have undertaken. If a person is accurate, he will be on time. He will know what to say or what to do. Confusion or disappointment

	will not be the end result. They will assist you in becoming victorious.
Truthfulness	Can what a person says be trusted? Are they truthful in word and deed? Are the things that a person says able to be proven? Is there evidence that will convince you that he or she is faithful? Has this person been truthful in your past dealings with him? Does he or she exaggerate to the point that the things that they say or do become meaningless? Have you witnessed or are there witnesses who could verify that what this person has said is in fact so?

If a man has not made good any of his promises, that man cannot and will not be trusted by those who know him. There are many of you who have made promises over and over again, but time after time you have broken your promises to your family, friends and others. This makes it very difficult for people to trust you. In fact even when you are serious about the words that you speak out of your mouth if you don't do exactly what you say you cause men to doubt you. I am sure that many of you who are reading this book have been labeled untrustworthy. Regardless as to how well you can speak, write, teach, preach or dress, if you are not trustworthy, men will not open their hearts, lives and minds to you. They will not support you. Nor will they want to have anything to do with you.

There is something that is often said about the individuals who make their living in the entertainment field. About singers, it is said, that a singer is only as good as his last hit record. It is said about actors that an actor is only as good as his last movie. A dancer is only as good as his last dance performance. For authors, it is said that a writer is only as good as his last book. This philosophy is what the world uses to measure success and failure. "You're only as good as..." A person must keep on trying to prove himself to people who have doubts about his abilities, gifts, talents, etc. Strangely so, this vain philosophy even has crept over into the minds and thoughts of feeble Christians who have not grown into maturity or become believers of God's Word. They completely overlook the fact that God is the essence of trustworthiness. "Hey, parting the Red Sea, the virgin birth, turning water into wine, was alright but that stuff is history. What about now? I ain't seen no miracles in my life! Those things are not helping me now! I need my bills paid! I want my man back! What are you going to do about that God?" Friends, God knows that we have more than spiritual needs that must be met. When you are hungry, love, joy, peace, gentleness, goodness, meekness and the other fruit of the Spirit will do you no good. You can be blessed on the inside and dying on the outside of starvation in the third degree. God promises in Philippians 4:19 to supply all of our needs. He made provisions for the spiritual and the natural. God wants you to be happy. His Word says that He WILL NOT withhold any good thing from them that walk uprightly. (Psalm 84:11). First of all the adage about an author being as good as his last is true in one very special instance. God is an author and he is as good as His last book which is the Holy Bible. This book is God's Word, His will and it is eternal. He says that heaven and earth will pass away but not His Word, not His promises, not His covenant. Can you imagine the stability of that? Something that cannot and will not change no matter how explosive the circumstances or no matter how fervent the heat or how deep the flood. GOD'S WORD PREVAILS!!

Heaven and earth shall pass away but my words shall not pass away.
Mark 13:31

For this they willingly are ignorant of, that by The Word of God the heavens were of old, and the earth standing out of the water and in the water; Whereby the world that then was, being overflowed with water, perished but the heavens and the earth, which are now, by the same word are kept in store, reserved unto fire against the day of judgment and perdition of ungodly men. But beloved, be not ignorant of this one thing, that one day is with the Lord as a thousand years, and a thousand years as one day. The Lord is not slack concerning his promise.
II Peter 3:5-9a

Another important thing that Christians should remember is that God should not have to prove to you that He is God and God all by himself over and over. The scripture did not say "Be still because I must prove to you that I am God over and over". It said, "Be still and KNOW that I am God". When proof is required of something, that means that there is some doubt involved somewhere and it must be cleared up by something considered to be evidence. God proves Himself to sinners and to baby Christians. He proves himself to the sinner who has no knowledge of the Word and God's abilities, to draw him unto repentance and salvation. He proves

Himself to baby Christians because they are not fully acquainted with what God is to them and all that he will do for them.

The word *prove* means: to show to be true or genuine as by evidence or argument; to determine the quality or genuineness of; to test; to establish the authenticity or validity of. Christians, by now you should *KNOW* that God is God. You should know that he will deliver, break yokes of bondage, restore what the enemy has stolen, prosper the fruit of your labor. How many times does He have to do the same thing over and over for you and you still don't quite get it! You are still wavering, still wondering, still walking by sight. Christians have a very bad habit of equating God's power and His thinking with that of man's. In fact, they will give more weight to the words of man than the Word of God. Why? Simply because man is visible and people are more willing to accept something that is perceived by the senses. People tend to believe that if they can see something, they are able to control that thing, such as people, circumstances, etc. The proving period is over with now for most of you. Now it is time to trust. After all, He has proven to you that His Word works. You've seen manifestations. You must know and seek after the one that has spoken the Word. If you don't know God, you won't know the validity of His Word. Proving is the first step to believing, but at some point, belief should turn into knowledge because of manifestations. There is a difference between believing and knowing something.

> *If ye continue in my word then are ye my disciples indeed; And ye shall know the truth, and the truth shall make you free.*
>
> John 8:31b-32

God Can Be Trusted 71

You cannot honestly say that you are free in a situation or circumstance until the truth of the matter is known. When you know a thing, it becomes evident through manifestation. When the truth is known, it sets you free spiritually, mentally, physically, materially, and financially. Now, some of you think you know the truth because you are a "bible toter" and a "scripture quoter". You have a scripture that you quote for everything and every situation. When questions arise, you reach into your catalog of scriptures and pull out the best one you can find. It does not change the fact that you gain actual freedom when that verse of scripture produces the results that you need and desire.

In the spirit, you get excited. You shout and give a little dance of "foot service" unto the Lord as David did. That is as far as it goes if you don't begin to walk by the verse of scripture that you have quoted and gotten excited over. Once you begin to walk, talk and live that verse of scripture, it will no longer remain just words on a page of the Bible. It will come alive in your life. It WILL change your circumstances. Then you can say, "Hey, I know the truth." "Formerly, I believed it and it blessed me within. Now I know the truth because I am free in my finances, my body, my life, my home, etc." Remember, that if a thing can't be seen, then it is not a "known" truth. It is only a fact of faith that you believe.

Remember the former things of old: for I am God, and there is none else; I am God, and there is none like me, Declaring the end from the beginning, and from ancient times the things that are not yet done, saying, My counsel shall stand, and I will do all my pleasure: Calling a

> *ravenous bird from the east, the man that executeth my counsel from a far country: yea, I have spoken it, I will also bring it to pass; I have purposed it, I will also do it.*
>
> Isaiah 46:9-11

God has made promises to men ever since the beginning, and as of this day, he has made good on all of His promises. Whatever he has spoken to man, he brought it to pass. Why? So that people would not think of him as they thought of their dead, idolic gods of wood, stone and gold. God can be trusted because He earned trustworthiness by making His Word good in the old testament. His Word is good in the new testament, and in your life as well as mine.

There are people who walk around looking pitiful, full of complaints about life in general. They think that they are making things better for themselves by complaining about the circumstances. They poor mouth God and continue to call upon him to deliver them from their troubles. This is something you can be sure of; we cannot rush Him by complaining. Your murmuring will not cause Him to act more speedily. God knows exactly what He's doing. He can see everything that is involved in the situation. Remember, "O FINITE ONE", God's wisdom, knowledge, and understanding is INFINITE. He has always made good on His promises. He brought them to pass in His own time. If God, moved whenever we say "I need", we would never have to exercise faith. God never promised that we would see the answer to our prayers immediately. He has spoken His Word to us and expects us to believe it until it manifests in our lives.

God Can Be Trusted

Throughout the old testament, holy men expressed their trust in Almighty Jehovah God. David was a prime example. In forty-nine references in the book of Psalms, David spoke of putting his trust in God. Why would he put his trust in a God that had never come through for Him?

The Lord is my rock, and my fortress, and my deliver; my God, my strength, in whom I will trust; my buckler, and the horn of my salvation, and my high tower.

Psalm 18:2

God spoke His Word and brought it to pass in David's life. Solomon said that you are to trust in the Lord with all your heart and lean not to your understanding. Isaiah stated his trust in God in Isaiah 12:2

Behold, God is my salvation; I will trust, and not be afraid; for the Lord JEHOVAH is my strength and my song; he also is become my salvation.

The three Hebrew boys, Shadrach, Meshach, and Abednego, trusted God in the face of danger, that of being cast into the flames of fire. If they come out of their test without a hair singed upon their heads, without a spot on their coats or the smell of fire on them, how much more can we trust God to keep us in the midst of trouble and uncertain conditions?

God's Greatest Promise

Christ hath redeemed us from the curse of the law, being made a curse for us: for it is written, cursed is every one that hangeth on a tree:

Galatians 3:13

For he hath made him to be sin for us, who knew no sin; that we might be made the righteousness of God in him.
II Corinthians 5:21

Wherefore he is able also to save them to the uttermost that come unto God by him, seeing he ever liveth to make intercession for them.
Hebrews 7:25

But now hath he obtained a more excellent ministry, by how much also he is the mediator of a better covenant, which was established upon better promises.
Hebrews 8:6

The next day John seeth Jesus coming unto him, and saith, Behold the Lamb of God, which taketh away the sin of the world.
John 1:29

In the old testament, we can read about numerous accounts of where Israel had to trust God to deliver them from the hands of their enemies. God, whose name is faithful and true, proved his trustworthiness each time. Just as he made a covenant with Israel, he also has a covenant with believers of this dispensation. God promised a deliverer, one who would save Israel and the world from the effects of Adam's transgression. Through this deliverer we would have redemption. Indeed God's greatest promise has been manifested in the person of Jesus Christ. Jesus redeemed us from the curse of the law by absorbing the curse and becoming sin for us. Therefore, he virtually became us and we became him. He was the substitutionary sacrifice for the world.

Since Christ became me, and I became him, I am now holy, pure, righteous and whatever else he is. When he became sin for us, he had to get rid of sin. After being put death on the cross, he descended into the lower parts of the earth and remained there for three days and three nights satisfying the demands of divine justice. He then rose from the grave and commissioned men to take the message of his redemption throughout the world. If a man believes, then he shall receive the promises. If any man doubts, he will do without.

The awesomeness of the redemption story is so very real today. Through redemption we were justified, (declared righteous) and right now we stand in the presence of God and holy and righteous. Oh, if you only could grasp the genuineness of God wanting to meet your needs and grant you your heart's desire! Can you trust Him today?

In conclusion, I would like to reiterate the importance of faith being instilled in all believers. Every born again believer can and will have victory in every area of life if we utilize faith to its fullest extent. The world's system will stress you up and ultimately kill you, if you carry around its pressures. You can overcome the world by believing that Jesus has already overcome it and that you are one with him. Whatever he has, you have also. Wherever he is, just say, "I am there also."

It is up to the pastors, teachers, evangelists, prophets, and apostles to present the message of faith to the children of God. "How can they hear without a preacher", is what the Word says. The preachers must remember that the fruit of what they preach will be shown in the lives of believers. If those who listen to you day after day, week after week are defeated, whining and lacking materially, physically, spiritually, and mentally, this is the result and the evidence of the kind of spiritual food that you are feeding them. If all believers were to hear the true word of faith, can you imagine the impact we would have on society?

Believers, you are also responsible for your spiritual development. If the word of faith is being taught, receive it without doubting and become that living epistle that God wants you to be. Break loose from the bonds of tradition! Don't be afraid to venture out and seek for the truth! If you really want to be free, God will direct your steps to the man or woman of God that is obedient in preaching, teaching and living His Word. Once you hear The Word, believe it and begin to walk in it. Then you will know with all confidence that God can be trusted. WHATEVER GOD HAS SAID, HE WILL DO FOR YOU!!

For additional copies of this book or an extensive listing of audio tapes that are available by Pastor Rickey Singleton

Please write or call:

Everlasting Message of Grace
PO Box 547
Dolton, IL 60419

Word of Faith Fellowship
12844 S. Halsted
Chicago, IL 60628
(312) 468-1060

These are some of the teaching series that are available for your spiritual enrichment:

Marriage and the Family.
Your Family Matters
Dating, Mating, Romance and the Real Nitty Gritty of Marriage

Your New Identity Series:
Sons and Daughters
Saints
Kings and Priests
Lovers
Heirs and Joint Heirs
Soldiers

The Believer's Authority
Ain't No Place Here For The Devil
Exercising Violent Faith
The Authority of the Believer

Praise and Worship
Set Free by Your Praises

The Grace Dispensaion
Restoration to Favor

Financial Freedom Series:
How God Supplies Our Financial Needs
God's Prospective on Earning Money
God's Prospective on Managing Money
God's Prospective on Giving Money
Reversing the Family Curse

Your Money Matters Series
How to Attack Lack in Your Finances
Prosperity for the Gentiles

Faith
- *The Mind: The Territory of Faith*
- *ABC's of FAITH*

High Hopes Series
- *How to Set New Goals*

Healing
- *Healing Is For You*

Evangelism
- *Tell Them That I Love Them*